D1124004

A NOTE TO PARENTS ABOUT BEING A BAD SPORT

Bad sports make winning less fun and losing more uncomfortable. Therefore, associating with people who are bad sports is definitely a losing proposition for everyone.

The purpose of this book is to teach children what constitutes a bad sport and a good sport. In addition, it teaches them how to be good sports instead of bad sports.

Reading and discussing this book with your child can help him or her be gracious when winning or losing. Because gracious winners and losers make more desirable playmates, teaching your child to be a good sport will increase the amount of positive play experiences he or she shares with others.

Playing games with your child in which you demonstrate appropriate behavior is an effective way to teach him or her how to be a good sport. Acknowledging and affirming appropriate behavior when your child wins or loses is another effective way to teach good sportsmanship. Refusing to play with your child when he or she is misbehaving and encouraging others to do the same is the best way to steer your child away from being a bad sport.

This book belongs to:

Paavali Douglas Horace

Published by Scholastic Inc.
90 Old Sherman Turnpike, Danbury, CT 06816.

SCHOLASTIC and associated logos are trademarks and/or
registered trademarks of Scholastic Inc.

ISBN 0-7172-8588-X

First Scholastic Printing, October 2005

A Book About
Being A Bad Sport

by Joy Berry

SCHOLASTIC INC.
New York   Toronto   London   Auckland   Sydney
Mexico City   New Delhi   Hong Kong   Buenos Aires

This book is about Lennie.

Reading about Lennie can help you understand and deal with **being a bad sport.**

People who do not win and lose graciously
are bad sports.

Bad sports are happy only when they win.
When bad sports lose, they often:
- pout,
- cry, or
- throw tantrums.

Bad sports sometimes lie so they can win.

Bad sports sometimes cheat so they can win.

Bad sports sometimes criticize other people so they can win.

They try to make the people they criticize feel bad about themselves and lose.

Bad sports are not good winners.

They act as if they are better than the people who lose.

When bad sports win, they say and do things to make the people who lose feel bad.

Avoid being a bad sport. Try to be a good sport instead.

Good sports realize that no one can win all the time.

They know that every person wins sometimes and loses sometimes.

They also realize that losing does not make you a bad person and winning does not make you a good person.

Good sports lose graciously. Even though they might not like to lose, they congratulate the winners.

When good sports lose, they allow the winners to enjoy winning. Good sports try to make the winners feel that they did well and deserved to win.

When good sports win, they try to help the people who lose feel good.

When good sports win, they are kind to the people who lose. Good sports encourage the people who lose to try again.

It is important to treat other people the way you want to be treated.

If you want other people to be good sports, you must be a good sport.